Men of Old

And Other Poems

For information address:
J2B Publishing LLC
4251 Columbia Park Road
Pomfret, MD 20675
www.J2BLLC.com

Printed and bound in the United States of America.

This book is set in Garamond.

ISBN: 978-1-954682-33-7

Men of Old
And Other Poems

By Evan Giddings

J2B PUBLISHING

Contents

A Fallen Soldier

Many have tried in song and verse,
To define the pain and hurt,
For a fallen soldier.

But mere words cannot describe,
The tear that's brought to the eye
For a fallen soldier.

They will say he fought with pride,
Right until the minute he died,
About a fallen soldier.

But there's a gap you cannot fill,
A gaping hole, which gives a chill,
From a fallen soldier.

There is pain for those bereaved,
They are consoled but still they grieve,
For a fallen soldier.

Many have tried in song and verse,
To define the pain and hurt,
For a fallen soldier.

Men of Old

Listen to the tales of men of old,
Whose stories lie yet untold.
Of Christians, pioneers, and warriors, too,
Who fought and died for me and you.

Marion with his tiny band,
Fought Tories trying to steal their land.
From his base on Island Snow,
Where the British dared not go.

At the Alamo, Bowie, Crockett, and Travis,
Fought for Texas independence.
'Till one by one they were all shot down,
While holding the fort in a mission town.

Stonewall Jackson, how he fought,
Until the night that he was shot.
Friendly fire from his own men,
To battle he never returned again.

Sergeant York with just one gun,
Captured a troop of enemy Huns.
Faith in God made his aim true,
And assured freedom for me and you.

Dolittle's raiders in their B-25s,
Bombed Tokyo, almost all survived.
The carrier *Hornet* transported them through,
And Liberty's bell rang forever true

Remember these men who fought and died,
Fighting to protect America's pride.
Pride in freedom and democracy,
Pride in nation and family

America

You may say, that today, freedom's in decline,
But if you listen to my words, I'll give you a piece of my mind.

Lady Liberty may have stumbled, but she will never fall,
She is still a symbol, standing strong for all.

Freedom not for the privileged few,
Freedom for me and freedom for you.

Freedom from fear inside your own home,
Freedom from those who'd do you harm.

Freedom to worship in just your own way,
Freedom to speak and freedom to say.

America! the greatest country of all,
America! with freedom for all.

Fire

A spark in the dreary darkness
A glimmer you couldn't miss
Then a flame
Slowly catching
Quickly building
Then burning
Then raging
Then roaring
A flickering beast
A flaming lion
Needing to feast
Never dying
Purifying
Not quite solid
Not quite liquid
Untamable flame
Giver of life
Maker of strife
Scarring the land
A reaching hand
Grasping food
Hunger never sated
Jaws of coals
Tongues of flame
Constant motion
Hot evulsion
Brighter than the midday sun
Faster than bullets from a gun
Leaving ashes in its wake
Pillar of fire
Column of smoke
Burning orange embers
A filigree of purifying flame

The Ranger

One lone rider on a dusty plain
A big roan horse with knotted mane

A six-gun gleaming from his belt
With seven notches on its butt

A Texas ranger from far away
Capturing bandits along the way

Into a cowtown he rode one day
Hot and dusty in the light of midday

From down the street a cowhand called
And then the ranger's gun drawled

The shot landed between the eyes
Then gunfire erupted from all sides

Bullets whizzed all around
The sound echoed in the little town

As the gun smoke cleared all you saw
Was the ranger standing, his gun still drawn

He mounted up, and rode away
And no-one ever forgot that day

The Stallion

Black mane swirling in the breeze
Hooves thundering on the dusty plain
Dark coat shining in the sunny blaze
Faster than the falling rain

Silhouetted against the setting sun
As he climbs atop a red-stoned Mesa
He briefly pauses his bullet-like run
To gaze back upon his chaser

No bridle or saddle shall hold him back
No rider to own or command him
No rope shall tie around his neck
No whip or lash shall sting him

He is a stallion, wild and free
As he roams the endless plains
Racing in the grassy sea
Never feeling any pain

The Falcon

A piercing eye looking low
Carefully searching the ground below

Soaring high on feathered wings
Searching for little yummy things

A pigeon perched on a rock below
Is finished by this flying foe

With talons of steel and a beak like stone
He floats aloft and soars to home

To his eyrie of sticks and leaves
To his chicks which eat like thieves

A piercing eye looking low
Carefully searching the ground below

Soaring high on feathered wings
Searching for little yummy things

The Sea

Rushing, roaring, roiling sea
Crashing, crushing, rushing
Booming loud and frightfully
Rushing, roaring, roiling sea
Whooshing wind blows madly
Darkened clouds shoot lightning
Rushing, roaring, roiling sea
Crashing, crushing, rushing

*This poem is called a triolet. It is an eight-lined poem with lines 1,4, and 7 identical; lines 2 and 8 indetical; lines 3 and 5 rhyming with the first line; and line 6 rhymes with the second line.

An Epitaph to Common Sense

Here lies poor Common Sense
To whose words we never gave two cents
He had very much to say
But we hardly gave him the time of day

He once was very active in school
And was used as a handy tool
He also worked in government
And even advised the president

He once was a very popular man
And had a book written about him by an Englishman
He was vital in the formation of our government
And helped lawyers with many clients

And so, as all good things must come to an end
Death has taken a very dear friend
He left two brothers named logic and wisdom
But it seems their time has nearly come

So rest in peace Mr. Common Sense
And pray that we will all repent

Emeralds

Emeralds
Inlaid in rock
Fruits of fields elysian
Subterranean wonders of God
Green gems

*This is called a cinquain poem. It has twenty-two syllables and five lines with a syllable count of 2/4/6/8/2 respectively.

Night Sounds

Wolves howling at night
An owl hoots in a tree
These are the night sounds
The trickle of cool water
Splashing in a mountain brook

* This poem is called a tanka. It is defined by its five lines which have a 5/7/5/7/7 syllable count. It is an extended version of a haiku poem.

Plants

The plant grows quickly
Green leaves spread towards the sunlight
Roots spread underground
Flowers bud and berries sprout
A feast for my eyes and mouth

Them in Mind

When God created the trees so tall,
He had the squirrels in mind

When God created the seas so deep,
He had the fish in mind

When God created the mountains so high,
He had the goats in mind

When God created the skies so free,
He had the birds in mind

When God created the plains so wide,
He had the rabbits in mind

When God created the deserts bare,
He had the camels in mind

When you yourself was still unborn,
God had *you* in mind

*This is a kryielle poem. It's divided into couplets and each pair of lines ends with the same word.

A Battle Sonnet

Marching bravely to the bloody battle
Walking or sitting tall in the saddle
Flags furled gallantly in the early breeze
Faces of mothers' sons looking towards battle
The faint sound of cannons reaches their ears
Then the crack of gunfire pierces the air
Bravely they charge into the fight
Drums roll as a battle cry rings loudly

The final shots echo in distant hills
Then as the moon rises all is quite still
Banners lie forsaken on bloody ground
Bodies lay lifeless for miles around
Monuments are built to honor the dead
We vow that these dead shall not die in vain

*A sonnet is a poem of fourteen lines consisting of ten syllables each. It is usually divided into the first eight (called an octave) and the last six (sestet).

The Ballad of the Sea

Sails full with the ocean wind
Bow cutting the briny foam
Fair winds they depend upon
To carry weary sailors home

A storm builds above their heads
As lightning flashes brightly
They lie awake in their beds
Thinking of wives and family

Waves crash across the deck
While thunder rumbles above
Rain pelts down their necks
As they work to head for a cove

A massive bolt splinters the mast
Cries come from below
Many a seaman breathes his last
As the rest heave and ho

The ship is crushed by the terrible waves
While men sink to their doom
A hundred men find early graves
In the sea there's always more room

*A ballad tells a single, dramatic event. It is a story-song and usually is written in four-line verses with the second and fourth lines rhyming.

Meet the Author

Evan Giddings was born in Fort Bragg, North Carolina where he still lives today with his mom, dad, brother, sister, and cat. He is homeschooled and his father is in the military. He enjoys backpacking, reading, listening to country music, playing Minecraft, and writing poetry.

Made in the USA
Columbia, SC
07 June 2023

17814806R00022